AL QAEDA
Myth or Reality?

Muhammad Abdullah

AL QAEDA
Myth or Reality?
Copyright © 2023 by Muhammad Abdullah

All rights reserved. No part of this publication may be reproduced, distributed, or transmitted in any form or by any means, including photocopying, recording, or other electronic or mechanical methods, without the prior written permission of the publisher or author, except in the case of brief quotations embodied in critical reviews and certain other noncommercial uses permitted by copyright law.

Although every precaution has been taken to verify the accuracy of the information contained herein, the author and publisher assume no responsibility for any errors or omissions. No liability is assumed for damages that may result from the use of information contained within.

Library of Congress Control Number: 2023901511
ISBN-13: Paperback: 978-1-64749-752-1
Epub: 978-1-64749-753-8

Printed in the United States of America

GoToPublish LLC
1-888-337-1724
www.gotopublish.com
info@gotopublish.com

O mankind! Be dutiful to your Lord, who created you from a single person, and from him Allah created his wife, and from he created many men and women and fear Allah through whom you demand your metal right, and do not serve the relations of family. Surely, Allah is forever a watcher over you. [Qur'an: 4.1].

Abu' Abd Arrahman Abdullah, son of Umar Ibn Al-khattab [ra] said: "I heard the messenger of Allah Muhammad ibn Abdullah [pbuh] say: Islam has been built upon five things – testifying that there is no deity but Allah and that Muhammad ibn Abdullah [pbuh] as his messenger; on saying salat [prayers]; on giving zakat, on pilgrimage to the Kaaba; and on fasting during Ramadan.

[Al-Bukhari and Muslim]

"War is a racket."

[Commandant Smedley Butler, United States Marine Corps, retired]

"Of all our studies, history is best qualified to reward all research."

[El-Hajj Malik El-Shabazz - Malcolm X]

Al-Qaeda 1998 –present leader Osama Bin Laden – Ayman al-Zawahiri. Ideology –Sunni Islam –Pan Islamism- Status designated on foreign terrorist organization by the US department. Designated as prescribed group by the UK Home Office. Designated as a terrorist group by European Union Common Foreign and Security Policy (CFSP).

Al-Qaeda [the base], alternatively spelled AL QA' IDAH and sometimes AL QA' IDA, is a militant Islamism group founded sometime between 1988 and late 1989. It operates as a network comprising both a multinational, stateless arm and a fundamentalist Sunni movement calling for global jihad. It attacked targets, civilian and military, in various countries, most notably, the September 11, attacks on New York City and Washington, D.C in 2001. The US government responded by launching the war on terror. Characteristic techniques include suicide attacks and simultaneous bombings of different targets. Activities ascribed to it may involve members of the moment, who have taken a pledge of loyalty to Osama bin Landen, or the much more numerous "Al-Qaeda-linked individuals" who have undergone training on one of its camps in Afghanistan, Iraq, or Sudan, but not taken any pledge.

Al-Qaeda ideologies envision a complete break from the foreign influences in Muslim countries, and the creation of a new Islamic caliphate. Reported beliefs include that a Christian-Jewish alliance is conspiring to destroy Islam, which is largely embodied in the U.S.-Israel alliance, and that the killing of bystanders and civilians is religiously justified in jihad. Experts debate whether or not the Al-Qaeda attacks were blowbacks from the American CIA's "Operation Cyclone" program to help the Afghan Mujahideen. Rolin Cook, British foreign secretary from 1997-2001, has written that Al-Qaeda and Bin Laden were "a product of a monumental miscalculation by western security agencies," and that Al-Qaeda, literally "the database," was originally with help from the CIA to defeat the Russians. Munir Akram, permanent representative of Pakistan to the United Nations from 2002 to 2008, wrote in a letter published in the New York Times on January 19, 2008: "The strategy to support soviet military intervention was involved by several intelligence, or ISI. After the soviet withdrawal, the western powers walked away from the region, leaving behind 40,000 militants imported from several countries to wage the anti-Soviet jihad. Pakistan was a left to face the blowback of extremism, drugs and guns."

A variety of sources –CNN journalist Peter Bergen, Pakistani ISI Brigadier Mohammad Yousaf, and CIA operatives involved in the Afghan program, such as Vincent Cannistraro, deny that the CIA or other American officials had contact with the foreign Mujahideen or Bin Laden, let alone armed, trained, coached or indoctrinated them. This runs counter to the account of Milton Bearden, the CIA field officer for Afghanistan from 1985-1989, who distinctly recalls the unease he used to feel when meeting the jihadi fighters: "The only times that I ran into any real trouble in Afghanistan was when I ran into these guys–you know there'd be kind of 'a moment' or two that would look a little bit like a bar scene in Star Wars, ya' know. Each group kinda jockeying around and finally somebody has to diffuse [sic] the situation." But Bergen and others argue that there was no need to recruit foreigners unfamiliar with the local language, customs or lay of the land since these were a quarter of a million local Afghans willing to fight; that foreign Mujahideen themselves had no need for American friends since they received several hundred million dollars a year from non-American, Muslim sources; that Americans could not have trained Mujahideen because Pakistani officials would not allow more than a handful of them to operate in Pakistan and none in Afghanistan; and that the Afghan Arabs were almost invariably militant Islamist reflexingly hostile to westerners, whether or not the westerners were helping the Muslim Afghans. According to Peter Bergen, known for conducting the first television interview with Osama: "Bin Laden... [is] a folk myth. There's no evidence of this... Bin Laden had his own money. He was anti-American and he was operating secretly and independently... The real story here is the CIA didn't really have a clue about who this guy was until 1996 when they set up a unit to really start tracking him." But as Bergen himself admitted, in one "strange incident," the CIA did appear to give VISA help to Mujahideen–recruiter Omar Abdel–Rahman.

[from Wikipedia]

Although the events of September 1, 2001 have left the realm of current affairs and entered history, Al-Qaeda remains an elusive phenomenon. As of this writing, the hunt for its leaders has led nowhere; Bin Laden and Zawahiri still show themselves with impunity on television screens worldwide, as people everywhere hold their breath in anticipation of another spectacular, devastating attack. The very nature of Al-Qaeda as an entity remains unclear, even when the metaphors drawn from astronomy have been exhausted. Whether one calls it a terrorist nebula or a galaxy, the terms point to the vastness of infinite, frightening space, but they also underscore our inability to conceive through which we are accustomed to understand political or religious organizations and internal relations at the time when the cold war began between Moscow and Washington was unfolding, according to a certain numbers of clearly defined codes, norms, and rules.

[*Al-Qaeda in Its Own Words* – edited by Gilles Kepel and Jean–Pierre Milelli –translated by Pascale Ghazaleh – General Introduction – Al Qaeda, the Essentials – Gilles Kepel – page 1]

"The supposed 'Science of Terrorism' served up by instant experts who crowd the television studios and bookstore displays props up wholly theories of the 'end of history and the clash of civilizations.' It offers precious little help, however, in grappling with the changes the world is undergoing at the beginning of the third millennium. The phrase, which belongs to the register of rhetoric, flatters anguished public opinion, but fails to enlighten."

[pp. 2-3 –ibid]

"After Bin Laden–the best point of entry to this universe and its most media-friendly incarnation, but one whose positions, as we shall see, have little theoretical depth – come two ideologies. The first, Abdullah Azzam, a Palestinian Muslim brother, herald of jihad in Afghanistan, and theoretician of contemporary worldwide, is known only to specialists. His thought, which is rooted in Islamic theology, is often obstruse, but it constitutes the key without which it is impossible to understand the central place of armed struggle in radical contemporary Islamism. The second, Ayman al-Zawahiri, besides being a media figure, provided the point of connection between the work of Azzam, assassinated in 1989, and the Islamist guerillas of the 1990's then theorized the shift toward 'martyrdom operations,' of which 9/11 was the apogee. He is undeniably the main thinker for this movement, having been nourished on the militant literature of Egyptian psalmists, whose course of action be radicalized, and occasionally evoking the messianic tones of protestant millennials, the broader group, the Italian Red Brigades, or the French group direct action. Al Qaeda's mental landscape ends with Abu Musab al-Zarqawi, the activist who took over the Iraqi battlefield at the cost of the atrocities attributed to him, meanwhile pledging allegiance to Bin Laden and Zawahiri. His contribution is important less for its doctrinal value than for its anti-shite violence–an innovation in comparison to the other texts."

[pp. 4-5]

In 1928, in Egypt, Hassan al-Banna founded the most important secret organization of Islam, the Muslim brotherhood. Within just a few years, it attracted millions of followers. In Egypt, the Muslim brotherhood became a state within state. In terms of secret power, Imam Hassan al-Banna was on a par with the king. At all times, the Muslim brotherhood has wanted to create an Islamic state based on the Qur'an and the tradition of the prophet Muhammad [pub]. Hassan al-Banna confided to one of his closest associates, with whom I spoke in Cairo; 'We need three generations for our plans —one to listen, one to fight, and one to win.' Hassan al-Banna did not survive the first; he was shot on an open street on February 12, 1949, by the secret police. Sayyid Qutb was the head ideologist for the Muslim brotherhood in Egypt; indeed, for the entire organization. He was forced to spend the years from 1954 to 1964 in labor camps and prisons of the Nasser regime. Pardoned for a few months, he was arrested again in 1965 and executed on August 29, 1965. His writings are now found throughout the Islamic world and constitute an important theoretical basis for the militant resurgence of Islam. The new, radical movement in particular are frequently based on Sayyid Qutb's ideas.

Zeinab al-Ghazali is the female counterpart of Umar al-Tilmisani. According to her own assertion, she heads two million women of the Islamic world. Her organization – the Muslim Sisterhood – is structured like the Muslim Brotherhood and directed in the same conspiratorial manner. In two long discussions in Egypt and outside the country, she informed mean about her organization. In her words: "members of the Muslim Sisterhood are the heart of the Islamic movement. Hassan al-Turabi in the Sudan and is now security adviser to the president. A lawyer trained in London and Paris and receptive to western influences, he leads the Muslim brotherhood in his country and is a member of the international committee, the highest authority in the movement. Hassan al-Turabi is gambling for time in the Sudan at president, hoping by doing so to achieve the goal of an Islamic state without the use of force, we spoke together in Khartoum. The most important Islamic thinker of Asia was Abul A'la Maududi. There is hardly anyone else without whom the orientalists so strongly associate the concept of Islamism, the transformation of the faith into a political direction. Radical Islamism, which is not far-moved from fascistic tendencies, was created in the explosive climate of Pakistan, and it is still practiced today by Abul A'la Maududi's fundamentalist party, Jamaat-e-Islami.

[*Holy War* - Wilhelm Dietl – translated by Martha Humphreys –pp. XIV-XV]

"In this cauldron, Bin Laden was revealed to himself. His collaboration with Abdullah Azzam, who had been welcoming volunteers to Peshawar since 1981, led to the creation of the Maktab al-Khidamat, service bureau into mid-1980s. At the beginning of the decade, the two men collaborated closely and had clearly defined roles: Osama financed the movement and may have served as a communications liaison; Azzam was the ideologue and party man. The events that took place in the middle of the decade upset the balance, however, precipitating divergence and therefore the creation of what later became Al Qaeda. The US strategy for Afghanistan, as defined by Zbigniew Brzezinski and other advisers as early as the Carter presidency, was to exhaust the Soviet Union by sinking in an Afghan quagmire, but without dealing the USSR the final blow that might incite it to pullout. The goal was to make the war drag on. In this perspective, the point, for the United States, was not so much to liberate Afghanistan as to make its occupation a costly endeavor for the soviets, and by 1986, it was becoming increasingly clear that the Soviets intended to pull out as soon as possible."

[p. 19]

"One of the characteristics of these online texts – their digital form is constitutive of the networking that makes up Al Qaeda's very substance – is our inability to identify their authors with any degree of certainty. In a universe where copyright does not exist, we cannot be sure that Bin Laden, Zawahiri, or Zarqawi really wrote everything that is attributed to them. The probability is higher for Azzam, whose texts were printed on paper before being put online – even if copyright has always been a relative fluid notion in the Arab world. Paradoxically, the information age telescopes here into the bygone era of manuscript production, before the printing press was invented."

[*Al-Qaeda in Its Own Words* – edited by Gilles Kepel and Jean-Pierre Milelli –translated by Pascale Ghazaleh – page 5]

In spite of the difficulty of finding one comprehensive scientific definition for terrorism, yet the public perceives terrorism as a politically or ideologically motivation action that targets deliberately or at least callously, civilian non-combatants, to inspire fear and to achieve certain political ends. Under U.S. law, an "act of terrorism" means any activity that [a] involves a violent act or an act dangerous to human life that is a violation of the criminal laws of the United States or any state, or that would be a criminal violation if committed within the jurisdiction of the United States or of any state, and [b] appears to be coercion, or [iii] affect the conduct of a government by assassination of kidnapping. Admitting the limitations of the above definition and being aware of the omittance of the whole subject of state terrorism, yet we can clearly see how far terrorism is from the noble concept of the physical form of jihad. We may briefly summarize the differences in the following

1. Jihad is to be launched by recognized and established Muslim authority, as a policy of the collectivity of the Muslims to deter aggression. Terrorism, on the other hand is committed by individuals or clandestine groups that neither represent the majority of Muslims nor did they receive any authorization from them.

2. Jihad is to be declared, while acts of terrorism are born in secrecy and executed as a deadly surprise.

3. Jihad is limited to combatants who reprint a real danger to the Muslim military, while terrorism is usually directed to the soft sport of innocent civilians in a non –discriminatory way.

4. Jihad is bound to the ceasing of hostility and accepting peace if the combating enemy includes to peace, while terrorism is launched against people who are at the same state of peace to start with. Hence, any confusion between the destructive of terrorism and the constructive noble concept of jihad should never be allowed. Such a confusion is a travesty of intellect and an insult to religion. [Jihad hathout]."

The difference between Islamic democracy and western democracy is of course the following: while the latter is based on the conception of the sovereignty of the people, the former is based on the principle of the caliphate [leadership] by the people. In western democracy, the people are sovereign; in Islam, sovereignty rests with Allah [god], and the people are his caliphs or subjects. In the West, people themselves make the law, in Islam the people must follow and obey the laws that Allah [god] communicated through his prophets. In one system the government carries out the will of the people; in the other the government and people together just translate Allah's [god's] intentions into deeds. In short, western democracy is a kind of absolute authority that exerts it power freely and in an uncontrolled manner, whereas Islamic democracy is subject to the divine law and exerts its authority in harmony with the commands of Allah [god] and within the framework established by Allah [god].

[*Holy War* – Wilhelm Diet- translated by Martha Humphries – pp. 43]

The emblem is as green as Muhammad's coat. Most of the space is occupied by two crossed swords, which have remained the symbol of power even in the era of the universal weapon, the Kalashnikov. "Be prepared for anything, counsel the words beneath the swords. Above this is a merciful book," it is stated on the title page only Islamic fundamentalists – in this instance, the Muslim brotherhood –could choose such a combination as weapons / the Muslim brotherhood was founded with very clear goals: elimination of all western influences in the Islamic world. Opposition to the relaxation of Islamic traditions and customs, return to the pure teaching of the prophet, and creation of an Islamic theocracy on earth. For the pious membership, this includes primarily the restoration of the caliphate, eliminated by Ataurk, as the highest political and religious authority, as well as more extensive social reforms. In an interview published by the newspaper al-Ahram, President Hosni Mubarak stated that the orthodox Muslims had planned a revolution in three phases, based on the model provided by Ayatollah Khomeini. Mubarak said that documents has been found, according to which the plotters [assassins of President Muhammad Anwar Sadat] wanted to spread their ideas by religious institutions and mosques. In this way, they would attract followes who would then be provided with weapons. After the proclamation of a theocracy system in Egypt, the plan was to murder the leadership class within the state, to occupy the ministry of defense; and take control of the mass media. To counter the radical Islamic virus, Hosni Mubarak met with the faculty of the 1,000-year-old Al-Azhar University, the highest institution for instruction in the faith. Mubarak demanded that the correct interpretation of Islam. Cairo newspapers quoted him on October 21 as saying: "Your task is the cleanse Egypt of fanatics and to protect the youth from religious confusion."

In a long article that was kept secret, Khalid al-Islambouli confided indirectly to members of the Muslim brotherhood shortly before his execution: "all who fight for the cause of Allah should meet under the roof of the parent organization."

Hamah is the city in which in February 1982 the horrible Middle Ages returned. In three weeks of heavy fighting between the population and the Syrian army, 24,000 civilians and 6,000 soldiers lost their lives. Approximately 10,000 inhabitants of Hamah were put into jails and internment camps in all parts of Syria. Most of them never returned. The regime of president Hafez al-Assad in Damascus once again avoided being toppled. What happened? The Muslim brotherhood has existed in Syria for thirty years, since the revolution spark of the anti-colonialist movement of Imam Hassan al-Banna spread from Egypt, but only since 1976 has the extremely powerful organization become a household word. The Syrian Muslim brotherhood raises the spearhead of opposition against Assad, who uses his whole family to sustain his rule by brute force. The Muslim brotherhood in Syria is ninety percent Sunni; they are oppressed by the minority sect of the Alawites [eleven percent], a branch of the Shiites. The long-suppressed rage against the Assad clan broke out for the first time on June 16, 1979. On that Saturday, Islamic attitude among the new group in power previously had only a series of small bombings and attacks to their credit.

[*Holy War* – Wilhelm Dietl – translated by Martha Humphreys – pp. 87, 103, 43, 131]

"The list of ministers, published on May 1, 1978, showed Taraki as prime minister and Hafizullah Amin as his deputy and foreign minister. Another deputy of the prime minister was Babrak Karmal. Together with the army, they had carried out the coup – at the behest of the Russians. Daoud was not the Kremlin's linking because in the last year of his administration he had been strikingly friendly toward Islam."

[p.293]

In the meantime, the wheel of Afghan history has ineluctably continued to turn. Muhammad Daous was overthrown on a

Thursday afternoon, April 27, 1978. Hours later, Radio Kabul announced: "For the first time in the history of Afghanistan, the last remains of monarchy, tyranny, despotism and the power of the old dynasty of the tyrant Nadir Shah has ended. Power is in the hands of the revolutionary council of the armed forces." Three days later, the democratic republic of Afghanistan was proclaimed. For the first time, the name of the new strong man was heard internationally: Nur Muhammad Taraki. He called his deed "true revolution." The list of ministers, published on May 1, 1978, showed Taraki as prime minister and Hafizullah Amin as his deputy and foreign minister. Another deputy of the prime minister was Babrak Karmal. Together with the army, they had carried out the coup – at the behest of the Russians. Daoud was not the Kremlin's linking because in the last year of his administration he had been strikingly friendly toward Islam. There was no danger of such an attitude among the new group in power. However, Taraki immediately set about realizing his conception of a secular state. A radical program of land reform caused the peasants to revolt against the government. The group loyal to Moscow also started to revamp the educational system and to make provisions for girls to attend schools. Such a reform went against the grain of the tribal leaders, and they withheld their approval. In their eyes, instruction by male teachers for the daughters of the tribe is more important than immortality - it is a sin against Allah and incompatible with the teachings of the Qur'an: at this point in time, activity among the Muslim rebels increased operating from Pakistani camps, the Mujahideen attacked in the border provinces of Kunar and Pakta. On February 14, the test of strength escalated when the religious fighters kidnapped the American ambassador in Kabul, Adolph Dubs. The Afghan police fought back brutally, resulting in the death of the diplomat and his four advisors aggravated the situation. By this time the number of Soviet troops in the country had increased. There were now more Russians in Afghanistan than there were Americans in Iran before Khomeini's seizure of power. In March

1979, ongoing resistance was directed against the Shurawi, the "Unbelieving Devil" as the Russians in Afghanistan are called by the Mujahideen. In the Afghan city of Herat, mobs of troops and the roused population attacked the Russians, reportedly resulting in the death of more than 100 people. Days later, the government troops managed to reconquer Herat. Approximately five hundred to one thousand people were killed. There was fighting in the provincial capital of Jalalabad, halfway between Kabul and the Khyber Pass, and in August 1979 there was unrest in Kabul. Once again, the Russians had to expect trouble with their Afghan leadership. Amin governed only by resorting to mass murder. One of these brothers alone had thousands of political prisoners executed without trial. An entire people were full of hatred towards the rule of no more than 3,000 communists, Barbak Kamal and his supporters resigned from the government in the summer of 1979 and went into exile, allegedly to Prague. In August, the military leader of the coup, Colonel Abdul Qadir, was put into prison, ostensibly because of his opposition to Amin, who let no one who might eventually be dangerous to him go unscathed. Because of the "Wild West" climate in the rough southeast, the kremlin banked on Taraki, whose immediate neighbor in the lower house of parliament was a certain Vasily Safronchuk, the man in charge of soviet policy in Afghanistan. Officially, Safronchuk functioned as advisor to the soviet embassy, but in reality, as is so often the case in Soviet diplomacy, his authority exceeded that of Ambassador Alexander Puzanov. He made certain that by late summer of 1979 there were 5,000 soviet instructors in Afghan administration. The Soviet armed forces took over Bagram, the air base north of Kabul, and their officers were in command, down to the company level. Months previously the order had been issued that every Afghan military plane have a Soviet pilot on board. The Afghan army of 80,000 no longer seemed sufficiently trustworthy to the Russians. The soviets themselves took a hand in combating the Muslim rebels. In the summer of 1979, they first destroyed the harvest, which resulted in attracting to the airs still more young men capable of fighting. Holy war was proclaimed throughout the country, and at times the provinces of Kunar and Paktia were completely conquered. Only the large cities remained in the hands of the government. An increasing number of soldiers and members of the administration went underground. Entire brigades [each consisting of 1,000 men], with all their equipment, including tanks, switched sides. The fighting increased in brutality – on principle, neither side took prisoners. Then came the historic December of 1979, the guerrilla war was in its annual winter lull. Even in the summer the mountains are virtually inaccessible, and winter makes the conduct of war there impossible. The western world stared in fascination at the first major challenge by an Islamic revolution: the seizure of hostages in the US embassy in Tehran. At the Muslims were still suffering from the shock of the occupation of the mosque in Mecca. During December, the Russians mobilized fresh troops along the northern border of Afghanistan and flew several thousand soldiers to Kabul. These were pure combat units, and they landed expressly at the civilian airport of Kabul, not in Bagram. By the end of the invasion, 85,000 members of the Red army, under the command of Marshal Sergei L. Sokolov, were reputedly in Afghanistan.

>[*Holy War* – Wilhelm Dietl –translated by Martha Humphreys – pp.298]

You may have missed this in the news but over the West African nation of Mali has been unraveling. There has been little attention in the mainstream media and the situation seems to move from bad to worse."

>[Bill Fletcher, Jr., *Mali and the Collapse of Nation* – M States - The Final Call, August 7, 2012]

"If top diplomats are right, the world's next inevitable war is in mail. A West African country where Al-Qaeda-linked militants have seized control of vast swaths of the Sahara."

[*Los Angeles Times*, October 28, 2012, Robyn Dixon]

Looking gravely across a courtroom in Afghanistan, 7–year old Zardana raised her hand and swore to testify truthfully about the night a man shot her in the head, shot her brother in the leg and killed her grandmother. "Yes, I do, and I'm not going to lie," said Zardana, wearing a lavender head scarf and fiddling with a juice box as her image was beamed by video to another courtroom in Washington state, where US Army staff sergeant Robert Bales is charged with 16 counts of murder.

[by Kim Murphy, *Los Angeles Times*, Monday, November 12, 2012]

In the United States today, the production of the books on terrorism has become a veritable industry: they do little to advance knowledge , but they provide a sort of transition between a reading of the world structured by the Cold War, in which the study of the Soviet Union constituted the principal discipline, and our president's difficulty in apprehending the multipolar world that followed the collapse of communism – dominated by a single superpower opposed by complicated, confused modes of resistance, insurrection, and violence. The supposed "science of terrorism" [served up by instant experts who crowd the television studios and bookstore displays] prop up wobbly theories of the "end of history" and the "clash of civilization." It offers precious little help, however, in grappling with the changes the world is undergoing at the beginning of the third millennium. The phrase, which belongs to the register or rhetoric, flatters anguished public opinion, but fails to enlighten."

[*Al-Qaeda in Its Own Words* – edited by Gilles Kepel and Jean-Pierre Milelli – translated by Pascale Ghazaleh – p. 2,3]

"In a universe where copyright does not exist, we cannot be sure that Bin Laden, Zawahiri, or Zarqawi really wrote everything that is attributed to them."

> [*Al Qaeda in Its Own Words* - edited by Gilles Kepel and Jean-Pierre Milelli – translated by Pascale Ghazaleh – p. 5]

"Thank you, your highness, for your continuing support of the global counterterrorism forum. It is a credit to your leadership that are now able to launch Hedayah, the first international center of excellence for countering violent extremism- a critical step in giving governments the tools to deny terrorists a foothold in their societies. Let me also express my appreciation to foreign minister Davutoglu and thank Turkey for its close partnership and strong leadership on building this forum into its vital, innovative platform. Finally, I thank all our colleagues around the table for your commitment to this forum and its long-term vision. Secretary Clinton sends her best regards and her continuing strong support for the essential work of this forum. We meet at a pivotal moment in our fight against violent extremism in a number of places, and we have made substantial progress. As a result of international cooperation, al-Qaeda is finding it more difficult to raise money, train recruits, and plan attacks outside the religion. Its leadership has been dealt serious blows. In Yemen, thanks to a combination of international pressure and national leadership, al-Qaeda affiliates now hold little ground. And in Somalia, al-Shabab has gone from controlling most of the country's south and central religions and almost all of Mogadishu to scrambling for places to operate. But serious threats remain. In the Sahel and the horn of Africa, groups are using terror to advance their agendas. For some time, al-Qaeda in the Islamic Maghreb has launched attacks and kidnappings form northern mail into neighboring countries. As violent extremists carve out a larger safe haven, they seek to extend their reach and networks in multiple directions. Our goal now is to take greater aim at these and other threats; to say ahead of them as they evolve and to put into place long-term solutions that will yield lasting results, because we all understand that long-term solutions are essential. We are know that repressive approaches often fuel the very radicalization they seek to fight and we all realize that we must disrupt the radicalization process by fostering opportunity, promoting tolerance, and amplifying the voices of men and women who have been victims of terrorism we need to build government capacities to take on threats within their societies through approaches grounded in the rule of law and respect for human rights – by reforming law enforcement and criminal justice systems, engaging with local communities, and empowering civil society. We also know that no nation can succeed alone – we must work together, as equal partners, with a shared commitment to pursuing a world with more opportunity and less violence. This work is extraordinarily complex progress is often measured over years rather than months. But we can't let that deter us from acting now. This forum is ideally suited to play a central role in our collective effort, alongside our bilateral partnership and existing cooperation – whether in the Sahel, the horn of Africa, or southwest Asia. In fact, it already is playing a central role. For example, the Sahel working group has brought together senior policy makers from across the religion to focus on border security and develop best practices for criminal justice. And later today we will adopt a plan of action on victims of terrorism, to help strengthen victims' associations and break new diplomatic ground by offering the first set of international best practices aimed at ending kidnapping for ransom. The two training centers we've set into motion will make significant contribution to counter global terrorism and the ideologies that fuel it. First, the new facility here in the use- Hedayan – will train police, policy makers. This time of year, which will help investigators, prosecutors, and other develop rule of law – based tools to prevent and respond to terrorism. We hope these facilities will educate a new generation of criminal justice officials who will themselves goon to change mindsets within their own institutions. When our countries and groups came together in January 2001, to discuss the idea for this form. We agreed that it should be an action-oriented platform - not another talk shop, but a place to find and share what works, nimble and tragic enough to address threats as they emerge. Now we must continue the work we have begun. My country remains strongly committed to the global counter terrorism forum. We consider this to be the central mechanism for innovate, civilian-led counter-terrorism cooperation. We will remain an active partner for the long term. We thank you all for your cooperation, your resolve and everything your countries do to defeat violent extremism and leave behind a safer world. Thank you."

[*Deputy Secretary of State William Burn's remarks at the Global Counter Terrorism Forum Plenary*, December 14, 2012 – taken from the council of Foreign Relations Online]

"Al-Qaeda is a terrorist network of Islamic extremists created by Osama bin Laden, the Saudi-born mastermind behind the September 11, 2001 attacks on the United States. Bin Laden was killed on May 2, 2011, in a firefight without the United States forces in Pakistan. The next month, an online statement announced that Ayman al-Zawahiri, the group's longtime no. 2, was taking command of the international terrorist organization. Independent specialist largely agrees that Mr. Zawahiri is not an inspiring model for young militants, noting his lack of combat experience, his long history of ideological squabbles and his abrasive manner and pedantic speeches. He inherited a central Qaeda organization that is under intense pressure, even as its ideology has spread and spawned dangerous affiliates in Yemen, North Africa, Somalia and elsewhere. In fact, the affiliates have gained in stature at the expense of the core al-Qaeda leadership of perhaps a dozen operatives, many of whom served for year as bin Laden's death accelerated this trend. Perhaps most significantly, the pro-democracy uprising of the Arab spring have left al-Qaeda's leader as a bystander to history. The ouster of Egypt's former president, Hosni Mubarak, a central goal of Mr.

Zawahiri's career, was carried out without him and by methods he had long denounced. The wave of Arab unrest reached Syria in March 2011, when an uprising that began as a peaceful protest movement slowly turned into an armed battle in response to overwhelming lethal force used by the government of President Bashar al-Assad. But in February 2012, American counter-terrorism officials said that a few hundred militants either tied to al-Qaeda in Iraq had moved into neighboring Syria to exploit the political turmoil, as the battle evolved into a sectarian war between a Sunni-dominated by the Alawite sect. By the summer of 2012, it was clear that al-Qaeda and other Islamic extremists were doing their best to hijack Syria's revolution, with a growing although still limited success that has American officials publicly concerned, and Iraqi officials next door openly alarmed. Evidence was mounting that Syria had become a magnet for Sunni extremists, including those operating the banner of al-Qaeda. An important border crossing with Turkey that fell into Syrian rebels' hands in mid-July 2012, Bab al–Hawa, quickly became a jihadist congregating point. The presence of jihadist in Syria accelerated in late joy in part because of a convergence with the sectarian tensions across the country's long border in Iraq. Al-Qaeda, through an audio statement, made an undistinguished bid to link it insurgency in Iraq with the revolution in Syria, depicting both as sectarian conflicts Sunnis versus Shiites."

[*The New York Times*, updated July 30, 2012]

Egypt – *misr umm El-Bilad*, the mother of all countries, according to an old song - is standing at the crossroads. The Alawites were founded in the year 872, and their first leader, Muhammad ibn Nasir, incorporated Islamic, Christian and heathen-gnostic elements into the faith. The French mandate authorities promised them their own state with Latakia as its center. For the sake of simplicity, they called them Alawites, taking the name from their deal, the stepson of Muhammad [pbuh] whose name was Ali. The four tribes of the Alawites still live in the vicinity of Latakia.

The powerful people of the county – among them Assad's family – all belong to the al-Matawirah tribe, which differs only in nuances from the religious community. Since 1973, the Muslim brotherhood has systematically prepared for the big exchange of blows with the "regime of the infidels."

[*Holy War* – Wilhelm Dietl – translated by Martha Humphreys – p.106]

The Osama Bin Laden-manhunt film "Zero Dark Thirty" came under fire Wednesday from a bipartisan group of senators who complained to Sony Pictures that the drama is "grossly inaccurate and misleading," because it suggests that torture held extract key information from a terrorism suspect. In a letter to studio chief Michael Lynton, Sen. Dianne Feinstein (D-Calif.), Carl Levin (D-Mich.) and John McCain (R-Ariz) wrote that the movie, directed by Kathryn Bigelow: "improperly establishes a connection between 'enhanced intentions' and 'key intelligence'. We write to express our deep disappointment with the movie 'Zero Dark Thirty'. We believe the film is grossly inaccurate and misleading in its suggestion that torture resulted in information that led to the location of [Osama] Bin Laden." Wrote senators, all of whom are members of the senate intelligence committee, which Feinstein heads. Through they stopped short of specifying what action they'd like from Sony, the senators suggested that they were hoping for a disclaimer of some sort. "Please consider correcting the impression that the CIA's use of coercive interrogation techniques led to the operation against [Osama]," they wrote. The senators' letter come on the heels of other complaints in Washington that the filmmakers may have had improper access to government sources or information while researching the movie. Financed by Silicon Valley scion Megan Ellison, the $45-million picture has given fuel to a long-running debate in Washington over the CIA's use of "enhanced interrogations" of terrorism suspects that were authorized during the George W. Bush administration. Congressional democrats have strongly condemned the practice as unethical and ineffective, and president Obama halted the use of such methods after taking office, Feinstein and Levin recently oversaw the compilation of an extensive report, endorsed by democrats on the senate intelligence committee last week, that condemned the use of harsh interrogation during the Bush administration and found that such methods did not lead to useful intelligence in the Bin Laden hunt or in other overseas missions, but they have not taken a position on "Zero Dark Thirty" until Wednesday. They were joined in the letter McCain, an ex-officio, nonvoting member of the intelligence committee. Unlike other republicans on the panel who voted against the report last week, the former POW has said that he supports its conclusion about the infectives of torture. "Zero Dark Thirty" opened Wednesday in Los Angeles and New York to strong reviews. It depicts the successful search for Bin Laden that began with a tip in Pakistan in 2003 and culminated in a nighttime raid in May 2011. The film begins with scenes of torture at a CIA "black site" – a secret overseas detention location – that yields a key piece of intelligence."

[*Los Angeles Times*, Thursday, December 20, 2012]

"The agency faces fresh questions about torture sparked by 'Zero Dark Thirty.' A decade after the last Al-Qaeda detainee was waterboarded, Americans still know little about what the CIA did to its prisoners, or whether it worked. President Obama decided against an investigation to hold accountable George W. Bush administration and CIA officials who conceived and conducted what he and others believed were acts of torture and criminal investigation, which ended last year with no changes and no public report. But now, a Hollywood movie has put renewed pressure on CIA officials to reveal whether simulated drawing and other harsh techniques elicited valuable intelligence, as the agency has long contended 'Zero Dark Thirty', made by Kathryn Bigelow and Mark Boal after extensive consultation with CIA officers, is sparking a new quest for answers, in part because it suggests that torture by CIA officers was instrumental in pinpointing Osama Bin Laden's hide-out in Abbottabad, Pakistan."

[*Los Angeles Times*, January 7, 2013]

"The Obama administration is preparing to ferry hundreds of additional French troops to the North African-American country of Mali, bolstering a rapidly evolving military campaign in the latest conflict with al-Qaeda affiliates. US officials said they also were making plans to send drones or other surveillance aircraft and provide help with aerial refueling of French fighter jets, which bombed columns of al-Qaeda-allied militants in Northern Mali for a fourth straight day Monday. The Pentagon's moves reflect growing concern in Washington about rebels' advances, and a decision by the Obama administration to back France's operation after months of inaction. French official said they had halted the rebels advance on Bamako, the capital, but insurgents later overran Malian forces in a town about two hundred miles northeast of the capital. Defense Secretary Leon E. Panetta, speaking to reporters during a trip to Europe, said the US was already providing the French with intelligence help, citing "a responsibility to go after al-Qaeda wherever they are." Defense officials said small numbers of US troops might be sent to Mali and surrounding countries but that they would be limited to a support role. "We have promised [France] that we will … provide whatever assistance we can try to help them," Panetta said. As the Obama administration winds down the United States long, costly war in Afghanistan, the focus of Western government's terrorism concerns has shifted to places such as Yemen, Somalia, and northern Nigeria. Once-stable Mali joined the list after Islamism rebels seized the northern half of the country after a military coup in March. According to US officials, the militants set up training camps and increased coordination with militant groups elsewhere in Africa.

[*Los Angeles Times*, January 15, 2013]

"It seems historically that wherever French imperialist go, American imperialist follow in seeking to oppress and colonize the people. Today is January 15, 2013, the birthday of Dr. Martin Luther King, Jr. He was assassinated in April 4, 1968. Had America decreased in violence or increased in violence, since Dr. Martin Luther King's assassination? Almost two years remain before a NATO-led international military force in Afghanistan is supposed to turn over full security responsibility to the Afghan military. But the Obama administration and its critics are already sparring over the size of the residual US presence that will stay in 2014. The administration indicates that it will amount to only a few thousand troops – some officials have even floated the notion that none would remain after 2014 – while its critics, including Republicans in congress, have insisted that at least 10,000 and three times that number will be necessary to prevent Afghanistan from backsliding into instability. We don't presume to know the precise number of troops that will be necessary in 2015 to ensure that al-Qaeda and associated groups can't use Afghan territory to launch further attacks on Americans, the rationale for the US invasion after 9/11. But the Times' David S. Cloud and Alexandra Zavis report that administration believe it could meet that objective with a 'light footprint' strategy – like one it has pursued in Pakistan – emphasizing commando raids and drone missile strikes against al-Qaeda fighters. Both the president and advocates of a large residual force insist that Afghan forces are improving their effectiveness. Ideally, that process will continue so that in 2015, the Afghan army can competently prosecute the war against Taliban insurgents without significant support from the US military. Meanwhile, it is to be hoped, the Afghan government will root out the corruption that has undermined authority."

[Opinion – *Los Angeles times*, January 15, 2013]

"At one point, we ended up talking to the son of blind sheikh Omar Abdel-Rahman, infamous Jersey City imam who plotted a day of terror from Manhattan. Another time reached the spiritual leader of the Palestinian Islamic jihad. Little by little, it became obvious that all these groups were coordinating their effort in a worldwide network. Then one day the phone rang, and we hit an absolute gold mine. The caller was a brave Sudanese who was a member of the republican brotherhood, a group opposed to Dr. Hassan al-Turabi's fundamentalist regime in Sudan. He was now working as a plumber in Brooklyn. He was in the basement of a building and had just come across scores of boxes of old records that were the property of Al Kifah Refugee Center, also known as the office of service for the Mujahideen, the predecessor to Osama bin Laden's al-Qaeda international network. The records had apparently been moved there after the World Trade Center bombing from Al Kifah headquarters at the al-Farooq Mosque on Atlantic Avenue. He wondered if we would be interested. We immediately contacted the FBI in New York and Washington. To our utter amazement, they said they couldn't do anything about it. The field agents were extremely interested, but when they ran it up to their superiors, they were told it wouldn't fly. We even smuggled out a few pages to pique their interest, but the superiors would not budge. Then we got word that the documents were about to be destroyed in about five days. So, we decided to pull off our own covert operation. Our Sudanese contact went into the building at midnight to do his job, carrying several large toolboxes. He then immediately emptied the toolboxes and filled them with documents. We met him at the rear of the building in a rented van. We grabbed the toolboxes, each containing about 4,000-5,000 documents, and raced off to a kinko's in Manhattan, where we spent all night feverishly photocopying the material. Then we would race back to the building by 6:00AM and return them to the plumbers so he could put them back before the building owners showed up for work. We did this for three straight nights. The papers contained financial records, address books, information about the fabrication of passports, and countless other materials showing the Al Kifah Refugee Center's involvement in the worldwide jihad movement. When we returned to the building the fourth night, however, our contact didn't show up. We waited and waited but by 7:00AM we were very fearful that something had happened to him. We left and found out later that something had triggered the building owners' suspicion and they had caught him. While we were waited outside, he was being questioned and threatened in the basement. He is a tough guy, however, and somehow got out of it. We ended up keeping the original records instead of copies. Altogether, we only retrieved about one quarter of the information that was there, but it was great material. We got thousands of leads. Nonetheless, I still think it would have been much better had the FBI gone in. In the main text, I have focused on discrete pieces of the puzzle, including the three most significant foreign groups on America soil: al-Qaeda, and the Palestinian Islamic jihad. In the following decade, a shifting cast of characters attempted a series of attacks on American targets."

[*American Jihad – The Terrorists Living Among Us* – Steve Emerson – pp. 22, 27, 29]

"Well, the correct answer is: Barack Obama is not a Muslim. He's a Christian. He's always been a Christian. But the really right answer is: what if he is? Is there something wrong with being a Muslim in this country? The answer is no, that's not America. Is there something wrong with some 7-year-old Muslim American kid believing that he or she can be president?"

[Colin Powell's *Defense of Muslims* - by Iman Mikal Sahib - Muslim journal – November 7, 2008]

"On the October 19, 2008 edition of NBC's *Meet the Press*, former secretary of state and chairman of the joint chiefs of staff, general Colin Powell endorsed senator Barrack Obama for the presidency of the United States of America."

*[Colin Powell endorses Barrack Obama on Meet the Press –
by Asia Ali]*

"France boosted its troops in Mali on Tuesday as armored vehicles arrived in the capital, Bamako, as part of a planned 2,500-strong deployment to battle Al Qaeda militants."

[*Los Angeles Times*, January 16, 2013]

"Throughout America's early history, Muslims have played significant roles as explorers of the Americans, as slave labor, on southern plantations, as patriotic servicemen in wartime, and as enterers and educators."

[*Muslim Journal* – November 7, 2008]

"French ground forces engaged in combat with Al Qaeda-linked rebels in central Mali on Wednesday, according to French new reports, as the newly deployed troops launched their first grounded operation in a battle to oust the militants. The reported fighting took place in the town of Diabaly, which fell to the Islamists earlier in the week and came under heavy French bombing overnight. Some unconfirmed reports said French forces had engaged in street battles there."

[*Los Angeles Times*, January 17, 2013]

"Islamists, militants seized a western-run gas field in Algeria on Wednesday, reportedly taking as many as 41 hostages, including seven Americans, in apparent retaliation for recent French airstrikes against Islamist extremists battling to overthrow neighboring Mali."

[*Los Angeles Times*, January 17, 2013]

"Rumor has it the [Obama] administration would like to pull out perhaps half of the 66,000 troops this year and almost all the rest in 2014, leaving behind as few as 3,000 personnel, or maybe none at all: talk of a "zero option" has been getting louder from the White House. Obama has a perfect right to decide that the cost of victory in Afghanistan are too high. But if so, he should level with us instead of insulting our intelligence by claiming that we have already won a war that shows no sign of ending any time soon."

> [*The Afghan Formula* –op –ed – by Max Boot – Los Angeles Times, January 17, 2013]

"The offensive by Algerian soldiers to free hostages at a natural gas complex has refocused world attention on the dangers of a lawless desert region bristling with gun-runners, smugglers, and a virulent strain of Islamic ideology. Coming days after French airstrikes on Islamist militants in neighboring Mali, the raid Thursday killed or wounded many militants and an unspecified number of western and Algerian hostages, the Algerian government said. To the west of Algeria lies Mali, where Islamist rebels have intensified their fight in percent days to overthrow the government, prompting French military action backed by American logistical support. To the east lie Tunisia and Libya, where revolution beginning in 2010 overthrew President Zine El Abidine Ben Ali in turns and Mohammad Kadafi in Tripoli. Since then, militant and radical Islamist groups, including Algeria's Al Qaeda in the Islamic Maghreb, have become more emboldened amid the political upheaval of new government. Western countries have grown increasingly concerned that North Africa could become a seedbed for international terrorism. It was the strife in Mali, however, that led to the militant takeover Wednesday of the western run compound. The Algerian militants, who belonged to an Al Qaeda-linked group called the Signed-in Blood Battalion, said they were acting in relation for French airstrikes against Malian rebels."

> [*Raid in Algeria Points Up New Worry* – Los Angeles Times, January 18, 2013]

"The commander of Mali's army is so confident of swift French and Malian military victory against Al Qaeda linked militias in his country's north that he declared that the war would be over in a month. Three militants groups –Anserine, the movement for unity and Jihad in West Africa, known by its French initials MUJOA; and Al Qaeda in the Islamic Maghreb, or AQIM – remain in the northern towns of Timbuktu, Gao and Kidal, according to Alexis Kalambey, editor of Les Echos newspaper in Bamako, whose journalists are filling reports from the north."

[*Los Angeles Times*, January 23, Wednesday, 2013]

Republican lawmakers failed to open new lines of inquiry on the deadly Sept. 11 attack on the U.S mission in Libya despite back-to-back grillings Wednesday of Secretary of State Hillary Rodham Clinton for a fuller explanation of the administration's response to the much-debated terrorist assault. Testifying weeks before she is expected to leave office, Clinton emphasized in consecutive sessions before the House and Senate foreign policy committees that there was a "rapidly changing threat environment" in North Africa, citing the recent terrorist attack in Algeria and growing instability in Mali, Nigeria and elsewhere. "We now face a spreading jihadist threat," she told the senate panel. She said the flow of weapons and fighters from Libya since the overthrow of Muammar Gaddafi "is the source of one of our biggest threats. We have to recognize this is a global movement," she said of group aligned with Al Qaeda. "We can kill leaders, but until we help establish strong democratic institution… we're going to be faced with this level of instability." In sometimes testy exchanges, republicans pushed Clinton on whether top administration officials missed warning signs of the terrorist attack that killed US ambassador Stevens and three other Americans in Libyan city of Benghazi.

[*Los Angeles Times*, Thursday, January 24, 2013]

"The brother of Al Qaeda leader Ayman al-Zawahiri on Wednesday sanctioned violence against the West in retaliation for the French-led campaign against militants in Mali, saying the US and Europe are "making jihadists."

[by Maggie Michael, *Press Telegram*, Thursday, January 24, 2013]

"The Jihadists storming in Mali and taking hostages in Algeria are harbingers of much worse to come. Osama bin Laden may be dead, but Al Qaeda in Africa now threatens an area twice the size of Germany. Want to fight terrorism? Fund family planning and education for girls."

[Malcolm Potts, *Los Angeles Times*, Friday, January 25, 2013]

"The militants came with gifts of dates, milk, peanuts, cookies and plastic prayer beads, extolling Islam and promising townspeople they wouldn't hurt them. They took over houses, unloaded truckloads of ammunition, food and water and ordered families not to turn away. They took down the national flag from the school and replaced it with a black Islamic flag. They blasted the concrete cross off a church. They wore turbans covering their faces like masks, but spoke gently, promising to pay for any damage they caused. When not shooting, they slept, ate, and prayed. The Al Qaeda-linked Islamist fighters seized Diabaly in a dawn assault on Jan. 14, three days after France launched attacks on militants elsewhere in Mali to destroy what it called the threat of a new terrorist state in West Africa, one capable of exporting terrorism to Europe and beyond."

[Robyn Dixon, *Los Angeles Times*, January 27, 2013]

"French and Malian forces on Saturday drove Al Qaeda-linked islamists out of a key in northern Mali, a major advance in France's campaign against insurgents in the West African nation."

[Robyn Dixon, *Los Angeles Times*, January 27, 2013]

"French forces seized control of the town of Kadai in northeastern Mali, the last stronghold in the country for Islamic militants, officials said Wednesday. The overnight offensive was the latest success in advances that have seen Al Qaeda-linked militants ousted from two major cities, Gao and Timbuktu, since Saturday, official said."

[*Los Angeles Times*, January 31, 2013]

"The recent terrorist attack at a natural gas plant in Algeria - which, together with the counter-strike by Algiers, left 38 hostages and 20 militants dead - has aroused fears that we are watching the resurrection of Al Qaeda, no longer just in Southwest Asia but in virtually every corner of Africa as well. British Prime Minister David Cameron reacted to the event in a way that evoked the days after 9/11. "This is a global threat, and it will require a global response," he said. "It wants to destroy our way of life. It believes in killing as many people as it can. There's little doubt that the Algerian terrorists are brutal, nasty people, but many questions about them remain. Are they a branch of Al Qaeda? Do they have global jihadists aims? Do they seek to destroy our way of life? It's vitally important that we understand these groups so that our response to them is tailored to the facts..."

[Fareed Zakaria, *World View Times*, February 4, 2013]

"France in particular has history... it doesn't want to repeat in Africa. French military missions on the continent have often been deeply resented for their explicitly political aims, including shoring up client strongmen. Malians seems to like the sound of not having the French around for too long. The limits France has publicly set for itself - "weeks." French foreign minister Laurent Fabius said the intervention – may help explain why French troops were welcomed in Bamako by legions of motorcycle taxis flying the tricolor from their handlebars. But if Mali has taught the world anything, it's that a whole new front of Islamist terrorism can rear up without many seeing it coming. And already, as the region recovers from the bloody hostage talking by allied Islamists in neighboring Algeria, there are signs that an early exit from Mali may not come easily for France."

[*Time*, p.22, February 2013]

The movie that resulted, "Zero Dark Thirty", which was no.1 at the U.S. box office in its first week of nationwide release and has been nominated for five Oscars, is in many ways as dispassionate a procedural as the hurt locker. Yet, it has become the most politically divisive motion picture in memory. Not only does it stage brutal scenes of American operatives practicing torture at CIA black sites in the wake of Sept. 11, 2001, but in the eyes of many experts, it also forges false connection between information gleaned by torture and eventually discovery of bin Laden's hideout. In December, senate intelligence committee members John McCain and chairman Carl Levin wrote a letter to Sony chairman Michael Lynton, calling *Zero Dark Thirty* "grossly inaccurate and misleading in its suggestion that torture helped extract information that led to the location of Osama bin Laden" - specifically, the nom de guerre of bin Laden's courier Abu Ahmed al-Kuwaiti. The senators also asked the CIA to disclose what access and information Bigelow and Boal received from the agency. According to a statement by Michael Morell, acting director of the CIA, which cooperated with Bigelow and Boal in the making of *Zero Dark Thirty*, the film "creates the strong impression that the enhanced interrogation techniques that were part of our former detention and interrogation program were the key to finding bin Laden, but that impression is false."

[profile Kathryn Biglow, *Time*, p.26, February 2013]

"On September 11, 2013, Americans were honoring the death of almost 3,000 victims who were murdered by Al Qaeda terrorists 11 years ago. The date borders on sacred to most Americans, yet on that very day, Egyptians attacked the American embassy in Cairo. They ripped the American flag to shreds and hoisted a black Islamist flag. The same day, terrorists attacked the United States Consulate in Benghazi, Libya. They murdered four Americans, including the ambassador to Libya, Christopher Stevens. The United States provided the military power to overthrow Libya's dictator, Muammar Gaddafi, last October. Ambassador Stevens was personally involved. He risked his life to help ensure the Libyans would have a more democratic government. Because of his efforts to promote democracy, Stevens became the target of a terrorist group affiliated with Al Qaeda. He knew about it and told Washington that his life was under threat."

[*The Philadelphia Trumpet*, December 2012]

"It was a mortifying week. We watched angry crowds protesting outside of American outposts throughout the Middle East and beyond. Violent mobs chanted, "We are all Osama." Structures were defaced or burned. Islamic banners were trying to focus on preparing for a Presidential election - and we got handed a new mini - 9/11. In the week after September 11 this year, Muslim anti-Western violence hit nearly 30 countries, killing about 30 people. Especially in the Middle East and North Africa, we witnessed a meltdown of order in country after country. It felt like the world was unraveling. The explosion of unrest sent a chilling message. For the past four years, the Obama administration has worked hard to reach out to the museum world-wishing Muslims a happy Ramadan; embracing the Muslim brotherhood; apologizing for things America did in the Middle East to defend against the Soviets half a century ago; criticizing America's response to the Twin Towers falling. When the Arab spring began last year, the White House embraced it, praising and supporting the empowerment of the Muslim street. September 2012 provided that strategy a failure."

[*The Philadelphia Trumpet*, December 2012]

Many French citizens support the country's military mission in Mali, which as of Thursday did not include any reported deaths of French troops, despite concern about possible retaliation by Islamic militants, polls show. About two thirds of respondents in several polls of French adults said they backed the Government's decision to send troops to the West African country, a former french colony, in response to a Malian government request for help in controlling Islamist's militias."

[Friday, February 1, 2013, *Los Angeles Times*]

"In some of his most expansive comments since his movie touched off a Washington firestorm, the screenwriter of *Zero Dark Thirty* defended his film as depicting U.S.'s use of torture accurately and said that a pending senate investigation brought him "chill." "We've been accused of defending torture because there are disagreements in some quarters as to exactly which detainee undergoing exactly which form of interrogation first produced the lead that led to Osama bin Laden and thus... We shouldn't have included it," Mark Boal said. "I can't understand the logic to that. If we let the torture out, we'd be White history. Interrogations were clearly part of how this lead developed."

['*Zero Dark*'s Boal Feels 'a chill', Thursday, February 7, 2013]

"The nation's vexation over the morality and legality of President Barack Obama's drone war has produced a salutary but hopelessly confused debate. Three categories of questions are being asked. They must be separated to be clearly understood. 1. By what right does the president order the killing by drone of enemies abroad? What criteria justify assassination? *Answer*: [a] imminent threat, under the doctrine of self-defense, and [b] affiliation with Al Qaida, under the laws of war. 2. But Awlaki was no ordinary enemy. He was a U.S. citizen. By what right does the president order the killing by drone of an American? Where's the due process? *Answer*: once you take up arms against the United States, you become an enemy combatant, thereby forfeiting the privileges of citizenship and the protections of the constitution, including due process. You retain only the protection of the laws of war - no more and no less than those of your foreign comrades-in-arms. 3. Who has the authority to decide life and death targeting? In war, the ultimate authority is always the commander-in-chief and those in the lawful chain of command to whom he has delegated such authority."

[Opinion - by Charles Krauthammer – *Press Telegram* - Sunday, February 17, 2013]

"The steady influx of Arab volunteers, who began to arrive in Iraq before the war and continued to do so after the fall of the old regime, brought indigenous Iraqi salafis from other parts of the Arab world. These Arab volunteers are generally active in the Tanzim Qaidat al-Jihad fi Bilad al-Rafidayn [the base of Jihad in Mesopotamia], which is led by Ahmad al-Khalayleh, a Jordanian who is better known as Abu Mus'ab al-Zarqawi. Although the role of Arab volunteers has been exaggerated, their impact cannot be denied. The Iraqi salafis espousal of the path of resistance, and the Jihadi influences of Arab volunteers, led to the complete radicalization of Iraqi salfism, reinforcing their rigidity and intolerance."

[*The Different Faces of Resistance among Iraqi Sunnis* - by Nasr Salem - *Crescent International* - December 2004]

"Thaksin has been blaming everybody from al-Qaida to Muslims educated in foreign countries for the southern conflict. He has also accused neighboring Malaysian Muslims, such as the Islamic party [pas], which is ruling Kelantan state, bordering southern Thailand, of funding the Pattani struggle."

[Thailand's Thanksin unfazed by condemnations after latest massacre of muslims - *Crescent International* – December 2004]

"It has long been widely recognized that leading officials of the Bush administration were determined to invade Iraq even before they come to office. But only a privileged few were aware of the details of the process by which the neo-conservatives dominating the White House took their country to war. In plan of attack, Bob Woodward describes how the U.S.'s decision to attack Iraq developed progressively, from a sort of a psychopathic fixation on toppling Sadam Hussein into a full military occupation. Woodward begin with Bush asking Rumsfeld, on November 21, 2001, "just 72 days after 9/11 terrorist attacks," Bush instructs Rumsfeld to "get started on this" and ask that "this be done on the basis that would not be terribly noticeable" [pp 1-2]. From this point onwards, Woodward sets out to inform U.S. of an extraordinary serious of meeting in various key U.S. decision-making bodies, including the White House, the National Security Council, the Pentagon, and the U.S. Army's central command in Florida, tracing the march to war in Iraq mainly through the development of war planning, both militarily and diplomatically, over sixteen months."

[Revealing account of internal American politics in the run-up to the Iraq invasion – by Nasr Salem – *Crescent International* – December 2004]

Most Middle Easterners who hate America, Al Qaeda being an important exception, still make both an intellectual and ethical distinction between America's domestic system of politics and its people on the one hand, the U.S. government and its international conduct on the other. It is for this reason that they might applaud, or at least not feel particularly sorry, if a U.S. military base or other facility associated with the U.S. government were attacked... while simultaneously disapproving of the... targeting of ordinary Americans as occurred at the World Trade Center and aboard the civilian airlines on September 11," writes Dr. Drake. Quite significant are her points on the Arab-Israeli, Shi'ites and Sunni regional aspect, as well as the role of

Al-Jazeera. Her analysis grows in significance when she gives the reasons why America is perceived by Muslims and Arabs as a controlling, hegemonic, arrogant and ignorant power. She then breaks down the faulty thinking [if that's what Dubya 'believed he was doing'] behind the statement, "You're either with us or against us."

> [Trying to explain how the world sees the U.S. - - Blaming American first: Inside the hatred of the United States in the Middle East and Beyond – Laura Drake, Ph.D – commentary by Mansour Ansari – *Crescent International* – December 2004]

"Three men accused of plotting what would have been the biggest terrorist attack in Britain since the 2005 London transit bombings were found guilty on terrorism charges on Thursday. The three British Muslims from Birmingham in Central England, were accused of planning to set off as many as eight bombs in backpacks in crowded places as part of suicide rampage. Although no date or target was set for the attack, authorities who secretly recorded conversations among the men arrested them in September 2011 out of concern that they posed an imminent threat. A search of their apartment turned up components for making bombs and instructions on how to build one, and at least two of the men, inspired by Al Qaeda and the Taliban, had gone to Pakistan for training in Islamic terrorist camps, authorities said. The defendants - Ashik Ali, 27; and Ifran Nasser, 31 – were recorded discussing the potential use of assault rifles and poison and putting blades on the sides of cars to mow down pedestrians. They expressed hope that their casualty count would eclipse that of the July 7, 2005 Suicide bombing of subway trains and a bus in central London, which killed 52 people. "These men were the real deal," Det. Inspector Adam Gough said. "They were committed, passionate extremists." Beale defended the decision to arrest the men though no weapons has been assembled or specific target chosen. "At what point would people suggest we interrupt, at the moment they're about to arrive at a shopping center, the moment they leave their home, the moment they've made perhaps their first device?" Beale said.

[*Los Angeles Times*, February 22, 2013]

"Plans to base unarmed American surveillance drones in the African nation of Niger highlight to Obama administration's growing concern about extremist influence in the volatile region. They also raise tough questions about how to contain Al-Qaeda and other militant groups without committing U.S. ground forces in yet another war. In the short run, a drone base would enable the U.S. to give France more intelligence on the militants that French troops are fighting in neighboring Mali. Over time, it could extend the reach not only of American intelligence gathering, but also U.S. special operations missions to strength Niger's own security forces. The U.S. and Niger in recent days signed a "status of forces agreement" spelling out legal protections and obligations of American forces that might operate in Niger in the future. Pentagon spokesmen George Little acknowledged the agreement, but declined Jan. 30 to discuss U.S. plans for a military presence in Niger. "They expressed a willingness to engage more closely with us, and we are happy to engage with them," said Little, adding that the legal agreement was months in the making and saying it was unrelated to the recent fighting in Mali. The U.S. has found some of its efforts to fight extremists hobbled by some African government, whose own security forces are ill-equipped to launch an American-style hunt for the militants yet are reluctant to accept U.S. help because of fears the Americans will overstay their welcome and trample their sovereignty. At France's request, the U.S. had recent flown 17 Air Force transport flights to move French troops and their equipment to Mali. Mr. Little said, "U.S. aircraft also are conducting aerial refueling of French fighter jets based in Mali, and those operations will continue. Other U.S. officials said the Pentagon is planning a new drone base in northwestern Africa – most likely in Niger – but the plans are not yet complete."

[*The Final Call*, February 12, 2013]

"No sooner had we moved off than we heard shooting behind us. It wasn't aimed at us, and it wasn't particularly heavy - just AKs being fired in bursts – but it was certainly puzzling. We pulled off the trail and went to ground while we waited to see who showed up. The firing stopped and we waited in silence for twenty minutes or so. It was so quiet and peaceful that I was beginning to think about putting a brew on, when I heard the sound of marching feet on the trail. We all froze absolutely still. From my position, I couldn't actually see how many there were but the amount of noise led me to suppose ten or twelve. For some reason, it occurred to me then how incredibly difficult it must be for the Soviets to develop a strategy to win this war: they were actually fighting against six major Mujahideen groups, several smaller ones and a number of little private armies, none of which coordinated their operations according to any kind of system."

[*Jihad - The Secret War in Afghanistan* – by Tom Carew – p.155]

"I went back to my sleeping area for a kip, puzzled at what they could possibly be talking back into Pakistan. The obvious answer would be wounded, but there didn't seem to be too many here. I got my head down for a couple of hours, walking when evening prayers were called. Happy that I'd suggested Abdullah that I might like to come with him to one of the closed caves. One of the fighters he was with looked completely pissed: a big sloppy grin on his face and unsteady on his feet. This surprised me; I'd taken these boys for strict Muslims, but if they were up for a bit moonshine and were happy to share and were happy to share it will me, then I was game on. Lead me to it! We got to the cave and they led me in, and I found where my team were hanging out. But I was wrong: it wasn't booze. In the center was a big pot and the Afghans were sitting around it, passing long, thin pipes to each other. So not opium. I sat with Abdullah and after few minutes, the pipe got round to us. He had a go, passed it to me, and I took a drag. Jeeesus! I'd never even smoked a cigarette, and I spent the next ten minutes coughing my guts out while the Afghans laughed at me in a somewhat mellow fashion. When I'd recovered, I sat there talking with Abdullah and Blue, but I could see that the lights were slowly going out in their heads, and after a little while, I made my excuses and left to get a proper sleep. I woke up with the call to prayer and sat eating hot naan and drinking tea while they made their devotions. When they'd finished praying, I made sure that my team got plenty of breakfast down their necks and then walked over where the mule-handlers were beginning to get everything loaded. More than anything else, I was anxious that they didn't forget about my cargo. Seeing me, the mule boss – the older afghan whom I'd seen talking Abdullah the day before - walked over and in perfect, almost accentless English told me 'Don't worry, old boy, we'll get your stuff loaded up in a minute.' This place was full of surprises. I stood watching as the mule handlers carried sacks of flour out of the caves and hooked them onto the backs of the mules, before carefully covering them with tarpaulins to waterproof them. I suppose they use it to make bread in the refugee camps, I mused, though they'd be better off transporting it as grain: you can't dry flour if it gets wet. Then the old light bulb went off again: of course, this isn't flour; it's fucking opium! There weren't any mules because they were all jam-packed with drugs. Fucking hell! Suddenly, the big firefight on our last day on the trial fell into place: an attempted opium hijack. I knew it couldn't have been the army because they didn't bring the gunships in, but a big robbery made sense: no wonder Blue didn't want to tell me. There was obviously a lot of cash value in this lot, and the Afghans were anxious that it should get through, to the extent that everyone was milling around like a mothers' meeting when we pulled out. Feeling fit and refreshed after a couple of day's good food and rest, I was looking forwards to the walk, with nothing to do but tag along at the back."

[Jihad - The Secret War in Afghanistan – Tom Carew – p. 176-177]

"I was woken by a female voice. 'Excuse me, you are Tom Carew, aren't you?' I struggled awake and sat up. Standing over me was a tall, thin and very attractive English girl, with blond hair and a deep sutan. I wondered momentarily if I was dreaming. 'Er yes, I am. Who are you?' 'I'm Kathy Blake. London asked me to come and debrief you about your trip over the border.' Loughlin was William's boss in London, but there was no way I could just start yapping to her without clearance from William. After all, I had no easy way of verifying who she was. 'I'm sorry you've had a wasted drive. What will you do now?' 'I'd better ring in for instructions…' None of these people were in my chain of command. I told London that I wasn't reporting to anyone until I'd either spoken to William, or received his instructions in writing, confirmed by telex from London. It was a stalemate and actually, I was in the right. London told me they'd get back to me, and ordered me not to leave the hotel. I turned to miss Blake. 'They're going to get back to me. What are you going to do?' 'I'm not driving back to Islamabad tonight; it isn't safe for lone women. I'll check in here and wait for instructions.'"

[p .181-182]

"I went up to William's room and found him wrestling with a telex and his codebook. The latest message from London was apparently telling him to supply an AK-74 to the Chinese embassy in Islamabad. 'Are you sure? We've got one AK-74 and I'll be fucked if I spent all that time collecting it just to hang it over to the Chinese.' 'That's what it says here… look, maybe the Hezb have got another one that they'll give you.' As we were chatting, Hekmatyar himself came into office. Although we'd only met once, he recognized me and asked how my trip went. 'It was fine, thank you sir. Everyone was very helpful and we got almost everything we needed.' 'Is there anything else we can help you with?' 'Well, now you mentioned it, I've been asked to obtain an AK-74.' Hekmatyar didn't know what it was, but when I explained he was very helpful. He had a quick discussion with two of his aides and then said, 'There may be one at my house. These two will take you there, and if we have one, you may take it.' 'Thank you, sir. That's very kind.' We hopped in a jeep for the five-minute drive to Hekmatyar's compound. The place was surrounded by heavily armed guards, Afghan and Pakistan, but we were allowed straight through. I followed the two Afghans across a small courtyard to an out building. When they opened the doors, I could hardly believe my eyes. The place was an Aladdin's cave of weaponry and ammunition: there were dozens of Kalashnikovs, together with DShKs, RPGs, grenades and everything else you could think of. I had a good look through the AKs, and eventually found an RPK-74, the light machine-gun variant of the AK-74, together with one magazine but no ammunition. I wrapped it in a blanket and the Afghans drove me back to my hotel. I took the RPK straight up to William's room and dumped it on his bed. 'Jesus Christ, what's that?' 'It's an RPK-74. Hekmatyar gave it to me.' I took it to my room and shoved it under my bed to stop him bitching, and then went back down to see him. It turned out that he'd got confirmation that were to deliver the RPK to the Chinese embassy, and that we were to take the rest of the gear to the Islamabad office the next day. I went to my room to pack a few things, then we went down to the bar for dinner. As we ate, I brought up the subject of the opium again. I knew now it was a subject that William didn't want to talk about. 'Tom, there are some things that's better not to know,' was all he had to say on the matter."

[p. 186-187]

"Here was quite an audience. Some I recognized: Loughlin and John Miley; others were introduced, like a U.S. marine corps colonel called Fred Fox; the rest remained anonymous. For the first couple of hours, William spoke and answered questions about his side of the operations: liaison with the Hezb; logistics;

and number of areas which I had no knowledge of. Then it was my turn, describing conditions on the ground inside Afghanistan, how the soviets were operating. Mujahideen tactics and so on. Late in the afternoon, I got to the opium shipments, but almost as soon as I said the words, three of the anonymous men got up and left the room. I stopped talking in surprise but Loughlin told me to carry on. 'Don't worry about them, Tom. They don't want to know about this part of the operation.' Surprisingly enough, Mangel was ready to go as soon as we arrived at the HQ, and directed us the short distance to Hekmatyar's compound. Once we were through the guards, we were shown up to the offices on the first floor and ushered into the great man's presence, where tea was served."

[p. 207-208 - *Jihad – The Secret War in Afghanistan* – Tom Carew]

"Can the president legally order a drone strike to kill an American on U.S. soil? Atty. Gen. Eric Holder Jr. wrote this week in a letter to Sen. Rand Paul [R.K.Y] that he could envision 'an extraordinary circumstance in which it would be necessary and appropriate' to use such lethal force. Those word touched off a heated debate Wednesday in the senate over when and where the president can order the killing of U.S. citizens designated as 'enemy combatants.' President Obama have said that targeted killing Americans must be governed by some due process, but they have resisted public disclosure of their rules. Until this week, the administration had refused to allow even members of the senate intelligence committee to read most of the legal opinions that justified the one known drone killing of an American, the attack on Anwar Awlaki in 2011 in Yemen. The debate burst into public view on Capitol Hill. On the senate floor, Paul filibustered the nomination of John Brennan to be the new director of the CIA, imploring colleagues to join him in criticizing Obama for refusing to rule out the use of lethal force against terrorism suspects in this country. Brennan has been a chief architect and defender of the administration's drone program. 'Are we so complacent with our rights that we would allow president to say he might kill Americans?' Paul asked. No one person, no one politician should be allowed… to judge the guilt of an individual and to execute an individual. It goes against everything we fundamentally believe in our country."

[*Los Angeles Times* - EST Thursday, March 7, 2013]

"My third infiltration into Afghanistan was paddy's fight, and the first one I'd done with a properly trained helper. I'd expected it to be much easier but in fact it turned out to be a huge waste of effort."

[*Jihad – The Secret War in Afghanistan* – Tom Carew – p.209]

"The FBI and CIA helped capture an alleged Al Qaeda spokesman who was Osama bin Laden's son-in-law and have flown him to New York City to face numerous terrorism related charges, according to U.S. officials. Sulaiman Abu Ghaith was taken into U.S. custody in Jordan, where he was stopped while being deported from Turkey to Kuwait, his native country, under a scheme orchestrated by U.S. authorities. He is believed to have spent most of the last decade in Iran. He has been providing information to U.S. interrogators since his arrest, said a former U.S. official who was briefed on the case. A federal indictment unsealed Thursday accuses Abu Ghaith of conspiracy to kill Americans, among other charges. It alleges that he 'served alongside' bin Laden from May 2001 through part of 2001 and appeared on videos to praise the Sept. 11 attacks and threaten further assaults."

[*Los Angeles Times*, Friday, March 8, 2013]

"My third infiltration into Afghanistan was paddy's fight, and the first one I'd done with a properly trained helper. I'd expected it to be much easier but in fact it turned out to be a huge waste of effort. Although we weren't going to cross the border until the next morning, the Afghans wanted us to move up closer to the border. Apparently, they told me, the Russians has 'eyes in the camp.' Well, maybe, but I though it much more likely that they were trying to keep us away from the opium store. We loaded our kit and our escorts into a couple of old Toyotas and set off along the track towards the border. We were still inside the camp when someone caught my eye in Jamaat-e-Islami compound. Darkie Davidson. We made eye contact but no move to speak or communicate with each other. It was SOP; we didn't need to know what the others were doing. 'Look, we either sort something out now, or we can go back to Peshawar and you can explain to Gulbuddin Hekmatyar why we aren't carrying out his orders.' Paddy and I had breakfast with William that morning. The operation had been aborted because U.S. satellite imagery had revealed that the helicopter had been stripped down. I knew from examining the wreck that this had happened at least a month before we'd got there. There were grass and weeds growing through it in places but for some stupid reason, this intelligence hadn't been passed to William until after we'd left. William's next statement provided welcome news. Something occurred to me. 'Oh William, I saw Darkie up at Parachinar. Should we send our gear up there for him to use?' 'Best you forget you saw him, Tom. He's on another job.' Fair enough. After my first Christmas with my family for four years, I was given instructions to move to the U.S. Air Force base at Ramstein near Munich, where I would be staying for a week. By now I knew that I was going to be with the Afghanistan operation for the time being, which gave me – and my wife, for that matter – a certain sense of security which you don't get from normal life at Hereford. At Ramstein, the whole Afghanistan operation was housed in a special, secure compound. We were hemmed in by mesh fences topped with razor wire, by floodlights, by dogs and armed U.S. military policemen. My first move, on arrival, was to get a special ID card issued at an anonymous security office and then I moved into the compound.

After passing through an area packed with computer terminals - which in 1981 was unusual and space-age to say the least – I was shown into conference room in the back end of the building. Here I met two of the original CIA briefing team, which had sent me to Afghanistan in the first place, colonels Miley and Fox. The purpose of this first meeting was to work out ways of moving weapons, equipment and ammunition into Afghanistan, and for the next few hours we talked through all the options available."

"While the business side of the [arms] deal was being sorted out, I began preparations for playing my part as the loadmaster. The Ice-Air plane was to be a DC-6 so I was driven to a hangar at the airbase where there was a U.S. military version parked up, painted all over in drab grey. My instructor was a big black guy, U.S. Air Force I guess, although he didn't wear any badges on his uniform, and over the next two or three days he coached me through the entire process of loading the aircraft, distributing the weight, lashing down the crates. I was also given a briefing on how to check through the cargo. The international arms market, and particularly the dodgy end of it - which this definitely was - is a snakepit; and if we got ripped off, well, it wouldn't be the first time that a buyer had paid hard cash for a few boxes full of scrap metal and used tractor parts. Buyer beware. I returned to the office where my escort, an American officer, took my passport away to get it doctored with some fake stamps on to look more like the rest of the crew's, then we headed back to the hotel to meet the other members of the crew. They were a cheery bunch of Icelanders, very pleased to have a loadmaster along to supervise the cargo side of the aircraft rather than having to share the duties between themselves. My cover story was that I'd been working out in Oman, loading skyvans for engineering and oil companies, but that I wanted a change back to Europe. It wasn't very good, but it was the best we could come up with at short notice that would explain my ignorance of aircraft, in general and European procedures in particular. Back at the secure compound, I was debriefed by John Miley and his sidekick, captain Johannsen. They told me I'd just taken part in Operation Mana, which was nice to know. When we'd finished eating, we wandered over to the hangar and watched some U.S. army personnel de-crating the missiles. As we watched, John told me that I was to return to Pakistan the next week and was to receive a full briefing in the afternoon. The afternoon after the first - and I suspect only - hijacking ever committed by an ex-member of the SAS, we convened the planning meeting for the next phase of Operation Faraday in a conference room within the secure compound at Ramstein airbase. The other participants were all Americans, and military too, judging by their haircuts. Not that it's a particularly good guide; it was mid-January 1981 and my hair hadn't been cut since October the previous year. The aim of the meeting was to discuss plans for training the Mujahideen. The U.S. army is nothing, if not conservative. That's how the Green Berets saw themselves working, and that was damned well what the defense intelligence agency wanted them to do in Afghanistan. What the Americans wanted was a classic 'behind-the-lines' training set-up - which fitted their tactical doctrine - but they wanted me to implement it. Their scheme saw a short period of very basic training in Pakistan, followed by a kind of 'on the job' training inside Afghanistan which would also see the introduction of the SA-7s. This was all outlined to me by John Miley. Now there was a period of waiting. We needed clearance - from Washington for the operation to go ahead at all, and when it came I would be going out to Pakistan to get it all started. In the meantime, I passed some hours in one of the gyms on the base, pushing a few weights either on my own or in the company of a small group of huge black bodybuilders who could pick up the most enormous loads with ease. The rest of the meeting was practical and run-of-the-mill: how could the operation be concealed from the Pakistanis? 'It can't,' I told them. Pakistani intelligence knows everything that happens in the border area. One point of disagreement that I'd had with the Americans all along was that they were keen to teach the Afghans the techniques of urban terrorism - car bombing and so on - so that they could strike at the Russians based in the major towns. Personally, I wasn't prepared to do that although, of course, I realized that eventually they would find someone who was. In any event, if the fact that the U.S. was sponsoring terrorism and teaching the terrorists how to do it leaked out, there would be hell to pay. Much easier, therefore, to keep it all tidied away inside Afghanistan under the cover of the fog of war. In Pakistan, or one of the friendly Gulf States, it was much more likely that the press would get wind of what we were doing and thus scupper it, but by next morning it was all changed. When I arrived in the office, it seemed that a deal had been done and that the Pakistanis were now prepared to allow very small groups to train in a remote area close to Parachinar and conduct live firing at a military range near Thal, provided that no explosives training took place on Pakistani soil. At last, we were moving in the right direction. Once again, we were going through all the aspects of my plan. The main concern of the American contingent was to speed things up. John Miley queried the spare periods that I'd left in the syllabus: why did I need them? 'I may not, but these Mujahideen will be an unknown quantity. You also need to remember that they are devout men: they need time to pray during the day. This is their jihad, not some handy intelligence opportunity. If you do go over the border, and are captured, then no one will be able to help you. Remember, you have left the army. If you end up in Moscow, then you won't be able to hold out for long. We'll look out after your family but that's it. Look, Tom, at the end of the day, we don't want them too well-trained; do you see what I mean?' I did, but he wasn't going to have to rely on them in the field. If I was going over the border looking for Soviet equipment, I wanted to be able to trust my team. As we wrapped the conversation up, I asked him about the SA-7s. 'They're on their way. We've got a couple of Egyptian instructors coming out to run the training. They'll join you when you've set the camp up.'"

[*Jihad - The Secret War in Afghanistan* - by Tom Carew - pp.209-251]

Allah has decreed, "I and My messengers will certainly prevail." Surely Allah is All-Powerful, Almighty.

[Qur'an 58:21]

"Training inside Pakistan was then taken, more or less completely, into the hands of the CIA. Groups of Afghans were brought to Scotland for training by ex-members of the regiment. It didn't take long for the Western intelligence agencies to realize that, in the Hezb-e Islami, they were backing the wrong horse. The rank and file fighters were fine but the leadership, it became clear, was more interested in jockeying for power and making money from drug sales than in fighting the Russians. Instead, when the covert military support effort was stepped up again in the mid-80s, and modern U.S. Stinger missiles were introduced into the equation for the first time, support was targeted at the group led by Ahmad Shah Massoud in the Panjshir Valley. At the start of the Gulf War, I went out to the UAE for another training task but by then, my time in the army was short: twenty-two fun packed years were over. When I think about Afghanistan now, it's with a sense of sadness and regret. The Afghan war was Russia's Vietnam: they couldn't sustain the losses they received there and maintain the arms race with the Americans; something had to give and in the end it was the communist system. The ragtag irregulars of the Afghan resistance kept the Soviets fighting for ten years but then let their victory slip from their fingers as the country fell under the control of the Taliban - a fundamentalist sect who were, in effect, the last men standing at the end of the war. At least the Taliban are Afghans, I suppose. The legacy of our intervention has been somewhat more dubious. The need to pay for the war led the Mujahideen to increase the production of opium tenfold, and Afghanistan is now one of the most important sources of raw material for the illegal narcotics trade. They no longer have to spend their profits on weapons and they are reaping vast rewards. There is also the problem of terrorism. The jihad in Afghanistan attracted Muslim volunteers from all over the world, all of whom received military training and fundamentalist indoctrination, and many of whom are now using their knowledge and experience to wage war on everything else they hate: Americans, Jews, Sunnis, Shias; whoever. It's a sad irony that bogeymen like Osama bin Laden acquired their skills as a result of the CIA's training programmes. It was a strange time on a wild frontier."

[*Jihad - The Secret War in Afghanistan* - Tom Carew - pp. 277, 278, 281-282]

www.ingramcontent.com/pod-product-compliance
Lightning Source LLC
LaVergne TN
LVHW041548060526
838200LV00037B/1194